Titles in the series:

Magnets	0 241 11206 0
Mirrors	0 241 11207 9
In the Air	0 241 11205 2
On the Water	0 241 11208 7

First published in Great Britain 1984 by
Hamish Hamilton Children's Books
Garden House, 57–59 Long Acre, London WC2E 9JZ
Copyright © 1984 by Julie Fitzpatrick (text)
Copyright © 1984 by Sarah Silcock (illustrations)
All Rights Reserved

Designed by Linda Rogers Associates

British Library Cataloguing in Publication Data
Fitzpatrick, Julie
Mirrors.—(Science spirals)
1. Mirrors—Juvenile literature
I. Title   II. Series
681'.42   TP867
ISBN 0-241-11207-9

Typeset by Katerprint Co. Ltd, Oxford
Printed in Singapore by
Tien Wah Press (Pte.) Ltd.

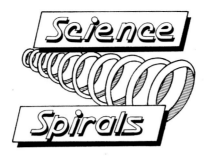

Mirrors

Julie Fitzpatrick
Illustrated by Sara Silcock

Hamish Hamilton · London

Remember

Most mirrors are made of glass.
Be careful how you use them.

Equipment you need for experiments in this book

Mirrors
Paper
Card
Pencils
Ruler
Scissors
Plasticine
A beaker
A cardboard box
Sheets from a wallpaper book
Glue
Blutack
Sticky-backed paper
Aluminium foil
Large spoons
Wooden or plastic letters

Mirrors

Look in a mirror.
What do you see?
You see a picture of your face.
What you see is called a
reflection.
Make a sad face.
Make a happy face.
Watch how your reflection
changes.

What happens when you look into a mirror?

Touch one ear with one hand.
What can you see happening in
the mirror?

Touch the other ear with
the other hand.
Whereabouts can you see the
reflection of your hand?
Keep watching how the mirror
reflects what you do.

Get ready to wink one eye.
Whereabouts do you think you
will see the reflection?
Wink your eye and
see if you were right.

Hold a mirror in front of
you and turn it slowly.
What things can you see
reflected?
If it is sunny when you do this,
you can make the mirror
reflect the sunlight.
Hold the mirror so that it
relects the sunlight on to
a wall.

What shape does the light
make?
Which way is the sunlight
coming into the room?
How could you make the spot of light
move up to the ceiling?

Put a mirror down flat on
a table.
Look down into the mirror.
Can you see any reflections
from the ceiling?

Hold the mirror up above
your head.
Look up into the mirror.
Can you see any reflections
from the table?
Do the things look the
right way up?

The Mirror Monster Game

You need ★ a beaker
            ★ 4 small pieces of paper
            ★ some Blutack

Draw a monster on one piece
of paper.
Draw pretty pictures on the
other pieces of paper.
Stick one pretty picture on
the front of the beaker.
Stick the other pictures
on the beaker –

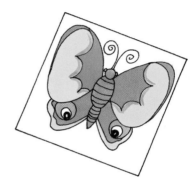

      1 on the back
      1 on the bottom inside
      1 on the bottom outside.

Keep the front of the beaker
towards you.
How can you use a mirror to
reflect the other pictures?

Ask a friend to look at the
pretty picture on the front
of the beaker.
Can he use a mirror to find
the other three pictures?
(He will get a surprise when
he sees the monster!)

7

How can you see what is behind you without turning your head?

You can use a mirror to
reflect things which are behind you.
Hold a mirror up in front of you.
Ask a friend to walk up
behind you.
Where do you have to put
the mirror to see your
friend's reflection?

Now ask your friend to walk
up behind you from side to side.
Where is the best place to
put the mirror so that it
reflects your friend?
Your friend might want to
overtake you.
Do you have to move the mirror
to see her reflection?

8

Drivers and cyclists use mirrors
to see the road behind them.
There is a mirror inside a car.
When the driver looks into it, he
can see a reflection of the road
through the back window.
What is wrong with piling up
things against the back window
of a car?

The mirrors outside a car
are called wing mirrors.
They help a driver to see
traffic coming up beside him.

How can a mirror help you to see round corners?

Fix a small mirror on to a ruler.
Take it and hide around a corner.
Hold your mirror out.
What can you see reflected?

Where is the best place to
put your mirror so that you
can see just around the corner?
What can you do if you want to
see things that are farther away?

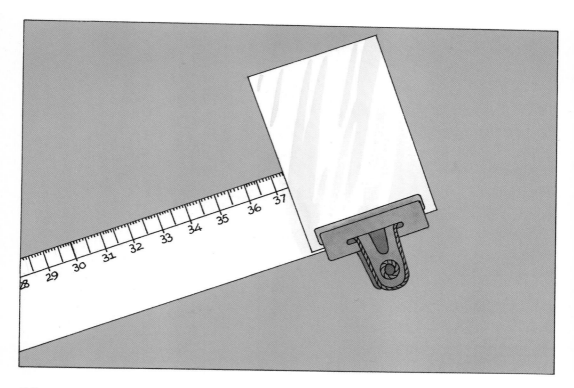

How to play Hunt the Hobbit

(A Hobbit is a strange
creature who will keep hiding.)
You can make one from plasticine.

Ask a friend to play this with you.
Get a box and put it on the table.
Ask your friend to hide the Hobbit
on one side of the box.
You must sit by the other side
of the box.
Remember how you used a mirror to
see round corners.
See if you can find the best place
to put a mirror so that you can see
the Hobbit's reflection.

Ask your friend to move the
Hobbit farther away.
What must you do to the mirror now
to Hunt the Hobbit?

11

How can you use mirrors to see the back of your head?

First hold a mirror in front of
you so that it reflects your face.
Pick up another mirror.
How could you use the second mirror
to reflect the back of your head?
A clue for you:
remember the Mirror Monster Game.
How did you use a mirror to see
the back of the beaker?

If you hold a mirror behind you
it will reflect the back of your head.
Why do you need to hold another
mirror in front of you?

Take the front mirror away and
see what happens.
The back mirror still reflects
your head, but now you cannot
see the reflection.

Hold both mirrors up again.
See how the front mirror
reflects the reflection of
the back mirror.
Move the back mirror to the
side of your head.
Keep looking in the front
mirror to see the reflection
of the back mirror.
A hairdresser uses two mirrors
like this to show you what your
hair looks like at the back.

Look at the reflection of
this line.
How can you use your mirror
to make the line look longer?
Can you make the line look
like a dot?

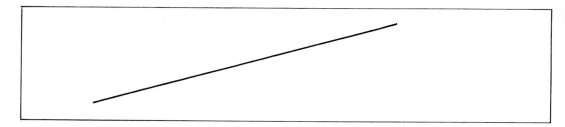

Use a mirror on these lines.
See if you can make some of
these shapes –

      a small square
      a large square
      a diamond
      a rectangle

What other shapes can you make?

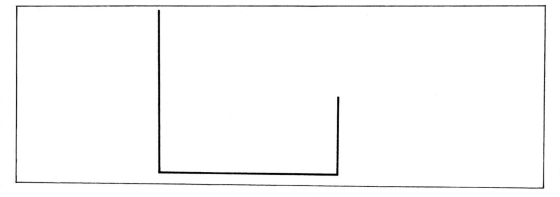

How can you make these half-shapes whole?

Can you guess what these things are before you look at their reflection?

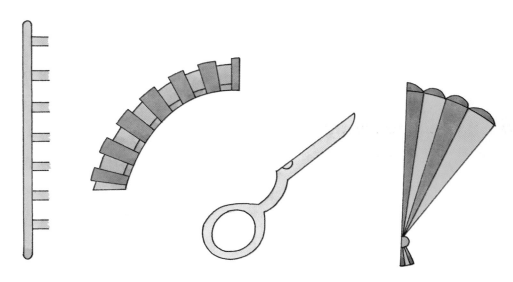

Draw some of your own half-shapes. Use a mirror and try them with a friend.

Get some sheets from a
wallpaper book and
cut them into rectangles.
Fold each rectangle in half.
Draw a shape, starting at the
fold line and going back to
the fold line.
Cut the shape out.
Open the shape then close
it again.
What do you notice about the two
halves of your shape?

Hold a mirror on the fold.
One half of your shape is
reflected.
What do you notice about
this reflection and the
other half of your shape?

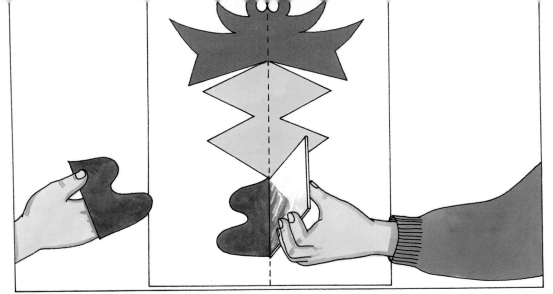

Draw and cut out lots of
different shapes.
You can stick them down to
make a totem pole.
Use your mirror on the fold
to look at the reflections.

Cut one of your shapes in half.
Choose one half of the shape
to stick on your totem pole.
Use your mirror to make the
shape whole again.
See if you can hold the
other half of the shape up
the right way so that it
matches the reflection.

Move your mirror across the
totem pole.
What changing patterns can
you see?

What happens to writing when you look at it in a mirror?

Hold a mirror on a piece of
paper with one hand.
Write your name with the
other hand.
Look at the reflection of each
letter as you write it.
What has happened to each letter?
Where is the first letter of
your name reflected in the mirror?

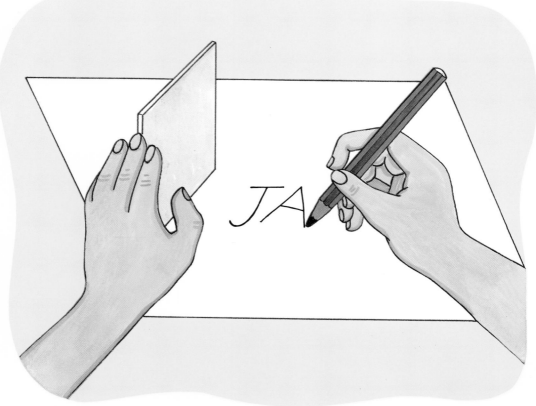

18

Look in the mirror and write
your name in capital letters.
Hold the mirror by the side of
each letter.
Do any letters look the same
in the mirror as they do on paper?

Find some wooden or plastic
capital letters and make a word.
Look at the reflection of this word.
Copy it on a piece of paper.
What could you do to each
wooden letter to make it
look like its reflection?

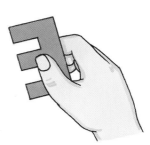

You would need to turn it over.
Are there any letters which
do not need to be turned over?
Do this again but this time
put the mirror at the top of
the word you make.

You can see one reflection in
one mirror.
What happens if you use
two mirrors side by side?
Fix two mirrors together with tape.

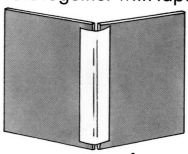

You need a paper square for
your mirrors to stand on.
Draw around a large square.
Cut it out.
Fold the square in half,
then into quarters.

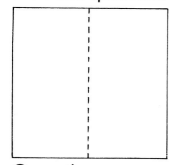 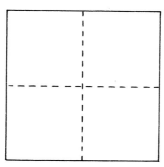 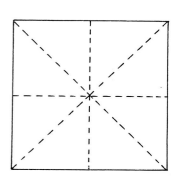

Open the paper out.
Fold the paper across from
corner to corner each way.
Open the paper out.
Choose two folds for the
mirrors to stand on.

Look into the mirrors.
How many reflections can you see?

Bring the mirrors closer together.
Does this make more reflections?
How many reflections seem to be
looking at you?
How many seem to be looking
away from you?

Open the mirrors out.
Where do you think you will
have to put the mirrors to
see one reflection of your face?
Try it and see.

Open the mirrors out and put
them along the middle fold
of the square.
Put a pencil facing the middle
of the two mirrors.
Look along the pencil and count
how many pencils you can see.
Write the number on the fold
at the end of the mirror.

Move one mirror in until
it stands on the next fold.
Move the pencil to the middle
of the mirrors.
Write down the number of
pencils you can see, as you
did before.
Do the same for the next
two folds.
What happens to the number
of reflections as your
mirrors get closer
together?

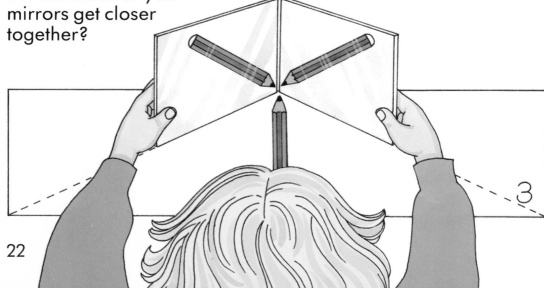

3

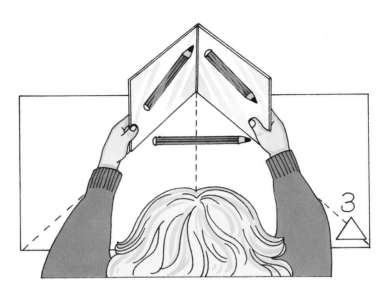

Open the mirrors out and put
them back on the middle fold.
This time, put a pencil across
the ends of the mirrors.
Look into the mirrors.
What shape can you see?
Draw the shape on the fold
at the end of the mirror.

Keep moving one mirror in, as
you did before.
Draw the shape that you
can see each time.
What do you notice about the
numbers and the shape
on each fold?
What is each shape called?

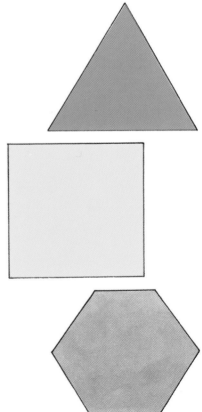

Get some sticky-backed paper.
Cut out some small shapes.
Stick one shape down on
the square of paper.
How many reflections can you see?

Stick some more shapes down to
make a pattern.
How many patterns can you see?
Are they all the same way round?
What shape is the whole pattern?

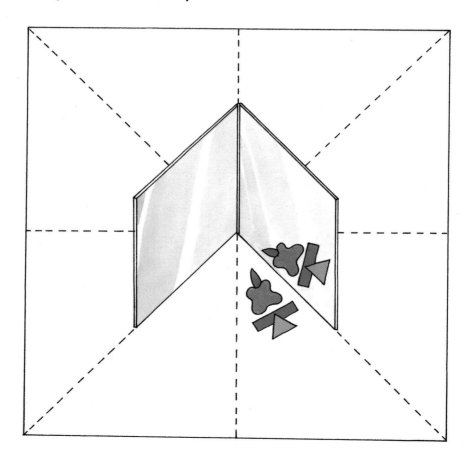

Put another mirror across the
ends of the two mirrors.
Tape the mirrors together.
(If you do not have another mirror
you could make your own.
Get a piece of card and cover it
with aluminium foil.)
Put the mirrors over your pattern.
Look down between the mirrors.
How many reflections can you see?

Turn the mirrors round on your pattern.
What different shapes can you see?
You have made a kaleidoscope.

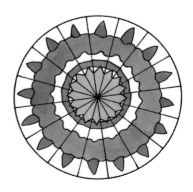

Where else can you see your reflection?

What is the same about
mirrors and all these things?
(They are smooth, shiny and
they reflect your face.)
What is different about the
shape of these things and
the mirrors you have been using?

Get a large shiny spoon.
Look into the back of it.
What does your face look like?

Hold a flat mirror beside
the spoon.
How is the reflection in the
back of the spoon different
from the reflection in the
flat mirror?

Are the things behind you
reflected in the spoon?

Turn the spoon over.
What happens to your reflection
when you look into the front
of the spoon?

Move the spoon towards you.
Does your reflection get
larger or smaller?
Does it became clear or
blurred?

Keep turning the spoon over and
looking at your reflection.
Can you guess what will happen
to your reflection each time?

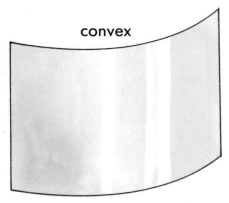

convex

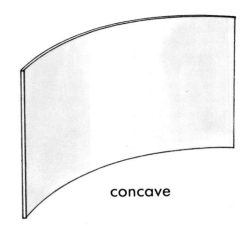

concave

Some mirrors are curved
like one side of a spoon.
A mirror with a middle curved
away from you is called a
concave mirror.
(You can remember this name
by thinking that it is like
going into a cave.)
A mirror with a middle curved
towards you is called a
convex mirror.
You may have some things in
your kitchen which are like
convex mirrors.

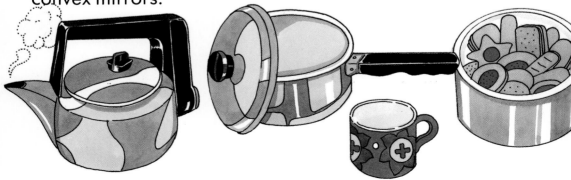

Sometimes convex mirrors are
used on sharp bends in the road.
They reflect traffic coming
round the bend for
other drivers to see.

What different sorts of mirrors
have you at home?
Keep looking for places where
mirrors are used to help us.

Index

Teacher's Notes

Plastic mirrors are the safest to use with young children.
E. J. Arnold and Osmiroid Educational supply double-sided unbreakable mirrors in various sizes.
Abbatt Toys provide larger double-sided unbreakable mirrors which children can bend to get distorted images.
Commercial kaleidoscopes can be obtained from Galt, Hestair Hope and Abbatt Toys.
Mosaics and symmetry cards can be obtained from most equipment manufacturers.

Storage of Mirrors
Mirrors really need to be stored vertically.
You may find a polystyrene packing tray that will hold them. If not, they can be kept in padded envelopes.
Teach children to hold mirrors by the edges.
They can see that if a mirror becomes smeary or scratched it will not reflect so well.